EXPERIENCING JESUS

JOHN R. VAN GELDEREN

EXPERIENCING JESUS

PERSONAL REVIVAL THROUGH THE SPIRIT-FILLED LIFE

REVIVALFOCUS
WITH JOHN VAN GELDEREN

Published by Revival Focus
Ann Arbor, Michigan, USA

Printed in the United States of America
ISBN-13: 978-0-9906693-2-6

Unless otherwise noted, Scripture quotations are from
the Holy Bible, King James Version.

Italics in Scripture quotations are the emphasis of the author.

Cover and interior design by InsideOut CreativeArts

To order copies of this book and other Revival Focus products
in bulk quantities, please visit revivalfocus.org
or call us at 734-531-9448.

To the Holy Spirit,
who as the Spirit of Jesus
testifies of Jesus,
glorifies Jesus,
and enables the saints to
experience Jesus

I am crucified with Christ: nevertheless I live; yet not I, but Christ liveth in me: and the life which I now live in the flesh I live by the faith of the Son of God, who loved me, and gave himself for me.

I have been crucified with Christ; it is no longer I who live, but Christ lives in me; and the life which I now live in the flesh I live by faith in the Son of God, who loved me and gave Himself for me.

I have been crucified with Christ and I no longer live, but Christ lives in me. The life I now live in the body, I live by faith in the Son of God, who loved me and gave himself for me.

My old self has been crucified with Christ. It is no longer I who live, but Christ lives in me. So I live in this earthly body by trusting in the Son of God, who loved me and gave himself for me.

GALATIANS 2:20, KJV, NKJV, NIV, NLT

CONTENTS

PREFACE

Did you know that if you're saved, then *the real you*—the core of who you are—is actually righteous?

Did you know that when you were born again, or regenerated, the Holy Spirit generated divine life within you? God's nature is now implanted in you, and it is righteous, holy, loving, good, and kind. Did you know that this divine nature in you constitutes the real you? This is the "all things are become new" of 2 Corinthians 5:17. Your body and soul are not yet all new, but your spirit is. There had to be a part of you made completely holy so that the Holy Spirit could move in and live within you.

Did you know that this provision is in you every moment of every day—and has been since the day you were saved? Did you know that this amazing provision was available even on your worst day? Did you know that, according to 1 John 3:9, the real you, as God's "seed," literally God's *sperma*, "cannot sin"? Obviously we can ignore this provision, and we *can* sin. But just as obviously, God's nature cannot sin. That is why 1 John 3:6 explains that the one who abides in Christ does not sin.

Did you know that *your real leader* is the Spirit of the risen, ascended, and enthroned Christ and that He moved into your life and joined with your spirit when you were saved? You have a personal guide, a personal generator—Christ in you—to lead and empower you for everything God calls you to be and do. The Spirit of Jesus in you is your real leader.

Did you know that *your real response* to the people and circumstances around you each day is the response of the real you to your real leader? The real you wants not sinful reaction but rather Jesus—every time. It's time to move past the noise of the world, the noise of your soul, and the noise of Satan's lies to your real response and start taking the provision of Christ in you and acting on it. As you do, you will start *experiencing Jesus*!

Interested?

ACKNOWLEDGMENTS

Many assist in the production of a book. I am grateful to the Lord for those who have assisted in this project. Each one has been a unique blessing. A special thanks to Gary Koski for his enhancing contributions in the early stages of writing and his help in computerizing the diagrams, to Rebecca Lawson for her outstanding professional editing with insight on the subject matter and her careful overseeing of the production stage, to Jennifer Cullis for her careful and thorough proofreading, to Rob Williams for his beautiful cover design and interior layout, and to Jason Chatraw for creating the e-book version of this book.

Also, a special thanks to my wife, Mary Lynn, and son, John, for their patience with me as I learn and keep learning to experience Jesus.

FINDING HOPE IN REDISCOVERING CHRIST

There's hope!" With tears in her eyes and hope in her heart, a Christian lady spoke these words to me after hearing the possibility of *experiencing Jesus* from Galatians 2:20.

In your Christian walk, would you like to go from being regularly defeated and surprised by occasional victory to being regularly victorious and surprised by a rare defeat? Is it possible? Many Christians are bound by the shackles of sinful habits. Qualities like joy and peace are far from them. Men in this situation fail to become effective leaders, and their leadership, if at all visible, is generally lacking in love. Women who have abandoned the hope of having rest and security are held in the grip of worry and fear. Young people beset with doubts about the future and their faith are tempted to turn from shallow religious exercises to hoped-for fulfillment in the world, but they find emptiness instead of answers. Can we do anything to experience the freedom of victory in our lives?

The answer is a resounding *yes*! There is hope! And thankfully, that which had to be done to bring us victory has already been accomplished. Are you interested? Consider the example of a man who, ignorant of his own need, endeavored to serve God and others while yet a stranger to victory.

J. Elder Cumming was a nineteenth-century Scottish theologian, pastor, and author. Educated in Glasgow before ministering in the city, Dr. Cumming was held in high esteem throughout the region and presented himself a formidable foe to those who differed from his views—and he dared to make those differences known. Perhaps hardened by the loss of his wife to a sudden illness, Cumming was keen to wield his intellect as a weapon. When challenged on issues of theology and church matters, he invariably answered the call and truly took pleasure in demoralizing opponents in a good debate.

Can we do anything to experience
the freedom of victory in our lives?
The answer is a resounding *yes*!

While touring Great Britain in the 1870s, the American evangelist D. L. Moody had the opportunity to meet and interact with

Cumming. The argumentative spirit that so often marked the Scot in his exchanges with others was glaringly apparent to Moody. Cumming was indeed a Christian; he had trusted in the blood of the Lamb for salvation. Yet Moody described this brother in Christ as the most cantankerous Christian he had ever met. Love was absent. Joy was missing. What could God do with such a man?

Obviously the Lord had started a work in J. Elder Cumming when he had found life in Christ his Savior. Now, years later, the Lord would continue that work, using systematic preaching at a summer Bible conference to open Cumming's eyes to a truth that would shake his neat theological grid. That truth? *Experiencing Jesus*—the very life of Christ living in him. Cumming was about to discover Christ not just as his Savior but also as his life.

In the summer of 1882, Cumming felt that he should attend a Bible conference. Ironically, of the many conferences he could have chosen in those days, he decided on the Keswick Convention—one he had been quite critical of since its inception in 1875, even though he had never before attended. Keswick (pronounced "KEH-zick") unpacked the truth regarding "the deepening of spiritual life" by addressing a particular theme each day during the five-day conference.

> The Lord would open Cumming's eyes to a truth that would shake his neat theological grid. That truth? Experiencing Jesus.

On Monday, Cumming's first day, the teaching exposed man's need through emphasizing the sins of the converted life—sins often glossed over by many Christians, such as resentment, irritability, and impatience. True to form, Cumming criticized the preaching of the day—typical cantankerous J. Elder Cumming. But on Tuesday the teaching lifted up Jesus Christ as the all-sufficient provision for man's great need. Cumming could not argue with this emphasis and returned to his room puzzled by the message of the day. On Wednesday the teaching pointed up man's responsibility to surrender in faith to Christ for freedom from the power of sin. By the end of that day, Cumming, whose theological grid was now shaken, desired some answers to riveting questions.

He approached one of the speakers, Evan Hopkins, commenting that since Hopkins was a theologian like he was, he would like to ask him some questions. Then Cumming fired away with all the savvy of his sharp mind. Hopkins normally responded to people with masterful explanations of biblical truth, but providentially he answered Cumming with only the very words of Scripture—words that the Holy Spirit knew Cumming could not argue with. Returning to his room deeply moved and under conviction, at first Cumming argued with the Spirit as to whether or not the issues he was convicted of were really sins. But soon he began to confess his sins—sins of the converted life. One layer exposed another, until finally Cumming's surrender to the Spirit's conviction was complete.

Thursday focused on the Spirit-filled life for victory, and Cumming now radiated with the glory of the Lord. The change in his countenance was observable to many. Deciding not to stay for Friday, which applied the Christ life to service, Cumming returned home, desirous of making matters right with a few brethren. Immediately after extending several apologies, Cumming became gloriously aware of the joy of the Lord on a level he had never before experienced.

The genuine change in Cumming soon became known, and he was invited to preach at the Keswick Convention annually for the next twenty-one years along with Handley Moule, F. B. Meyer, A. J. Gordon, A. T. Pierson, and G. Campbell Morgan, to name a few. Interestingly, when Moody returned to Glasgow nine years after Cumming's first Keswick Convention, so real was the continuing transformation in the Scottish minister's life that Moody commented, "Whatever has happened to Cumming? I have never seen a man so altered, so full of the love of God."[1] Is this not a radical transformation? Is it not personal revival?

> "Whatever has happened to Cumming? I have never seen a man so altered, so full of the love of God." Cumming had discovered the possibility of *experiencing Jesus*.

How could J. Elder Cumming go from being such a cantankerous Christian to one so full of the love of God? Cumming had discovered the possibility of *experiencing Jesus*—the reality of the Christ life, the Spirit-filled life. He had been filled by the Spirit with the very life of Christ. Sure, Cumming had already been familiar with the command of Ephesians 5:18 to be filled with the Spirit, but at the turning point in his life, that which God commanded became his actual experience. When Cumming accessed Christ's life, he accessed love, for the fruit of the Spirit of Jesus is love. He did not earn merit with God or somehow prove himself worthy. He saw in himself no good thing but in his Savior the grace and power that would effect a mighty change. By faith he began to experience Jesus in a new way. This truly is life again—revival on the personal level.

If this cantankerous Christian, stubborn and set in his ways, could be transformed into a genuine loving Christian, certainly there is hope for you and me. Galatians 2:20, a verse of but a few lines, states the truth of this glorious hope. Since Jesus Christ lives in the believer, we can and must by faith experience His victorious life. What makes this possible? Let's dig in to this goldmine text of Scripture in the next four chapters to discover and explore four important veins of truth.

SET FREE:
THE LIBERATION OF CRUCIFIXION

I am crucified with Christ.

GALATIANS 2:20

Scripture insists that all have sinned and fallen short of God's perfection. The problem this creates for us is that God's justice affirms that the just penalty for sin is death— meaning separation from God forever in hell.

The Bible also declares, thankfully, that Jesus Christ was crucified, suffering death to satisfy the penalty for sin so that sinners might have life in Him. Having shed His blood for the forgiveness of sins, Jesus rose from the dead and is now seated at the right hand of the Father in heaven. The work of redemption has been finished. Jesus died once for all and now lives evermore, and He promises eternal life to all who believe on Him. Thus Christ made a way for our problem of sin and its penalty to be resolved.

All this has been recorded so that people throughout the ages might understand the problem of sin, the penalty it brings, and the payment Jesus made for it. To receive forgiveness for sin and the promise of eternal life, we must agree with the Word of God on these matters and make a decision of faith to depend on Jesus' work on the cross and nothing else. A sinner becomes a believer by simply depending on the Lord for salvation, believing that the Lord is able and will do as He has promised. Have you made this decision of faith in Jesus Christ? Before you can experience Jesus, you must first receive Jesus by faith.

If we are children of God,
then these words are true of us:
"I have been crucified with Christ."

This message of salvation necessarily speaks of Christ's crucifixion. Jesus had to die to save us. Galatians 2:20 reintroduces His death but focuses it on the believer who has already trusted Christ. The focus here is not on Christ's death for us but on our death "with Christ." "I am [have been] crucified with Christ" plainly states the first vein of truth in this present study.

If we are children of God, then the fact identified by these words is true of us: we can and must say, "I have been crucified with Christ." As believers, God identifies us in Christ's death, and we must do the same. But what does this mean, and what is the intended impact of this on us as believers? Let's examine some vital questions.

WHAT PART OF US WAS "KILLED"?

Every believer in Jesus has been "crucified with Christ." But crucifixion is all about death—so what part of us was killed?

Before salvation, each of us consisted of a body, which housed the soul, which housed the spirit. This three-part makeup is depicted here in a circle diagram (see figure 1). Of these three parts, one had to die when we were crucified with Christ.

Physical death involves the two outermost elements—body and soul—and occurs when the

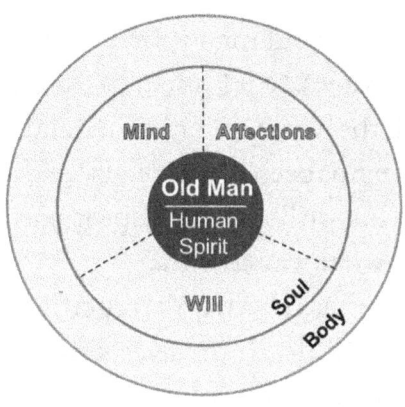

FIGURE 1: Unregenerate Man
Spirit, Soul, and Body

soul is separated from the body. Since you are reading this, it is safe to conclude that you have not died physically! Obviously, then, this matter of crucifixion with Christ cannot be a body and soul issue. Only one part of us remains as a possibility: our human spirit.

In fact, Romans 6 labels this spirit part of us that was crucified as the "old man." In a parallel phrase the death certificate for this part of us reads, "Our old man is [was] crucified with him" (Rom. 6:6). Our human spirits are person-ified with the wording "old man," and since our souls have not been separated from our bodies and are thus still alive, the spirit part of us is expressly what was crucified.

Remember, the word "crucified" speaks to death, and death involves separation. But separation necessitates a previous union or relationship between two entities. Our human spirits have been separated from something, but from what?

FROM WHAT WAS OUR OLD MAN SEPARATED?

The words "we, that are dead [we who died] to sin," which describe the justified in Romans 6:2, tell us from what entity our spirits were separated. Plainly, we have been separated from what the Scripture labels "sin."

Note that the word "sin" is singular. This passage in Romans 6 is not stating that we have been separated from *sins*, the collection of individual transgressions that Paul emphasized in Romans 1–5 when expounding justification by faith, which delivers us from the penalty for sin. Our separation is from *sin*, which Romans 6–8 emphasizes as it expounds sanctification by faith that delivers from the power of sin. This reference to sin in the singular is what Paul describes as sin that dwells in us (see Rom. 7:17, 20), or simply *indwelling sin*—our inward influence toward sins. Thus, the relationship that ended through death when we were crucified with Christ is this union with indwelling sin. Let's consider this in more detail.

Prior to salvation, we "were dead in trespasses and sins" (Eph. 2:1). The word "dead" here does not indicate the unanimated state of physical death, since obviously a corpse cannot revel "in trespasses and sins." The idea is that our human spirits, the *old man*, were previously dead to God. They were separated from Him. As such, they were "alienated from the life of God" (Eph. 4:18). But at the same time that our human spirits were separated from God, they were also alive to, or in union with, sin. They were joined to indwelling sin. Scripturally, indwelling sin is personified as a master to be served (see Rom. 6:6). Thus our *old man* was in a dreadful relationship of servitude with indwelling sin positioned as our *old master* (see figure 2). We were chained and shackled, as it were, to the taskmaster of indwelling sin!

This union with indwelling sin defiles everything an unregenerate (unsaved) person does. Knowing this allows us to understand why the Scripture condemns even seemingly moral actions, saying things like, "The plowing of the wicked, is sin" (Prov. 21:4). Even the most noble and charitable humanitarian efforts undertaken while in service to the old master find no acceptance with God, because they are defiled by this relationship that produces tainted motives and self-dependence. The self-righteousness that such works yield is "as filthy rags" in God's sight (Isa. 64:6) and falls "short of the glory of God" (Rom. 3:23).

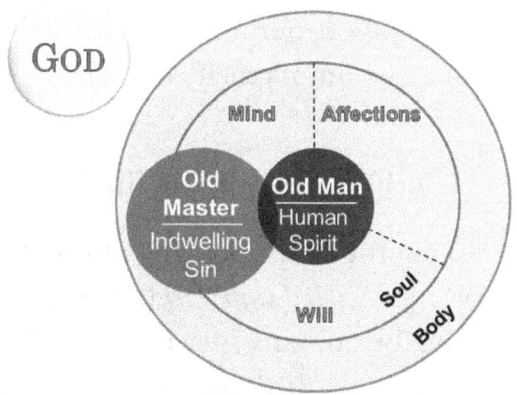

FIGURE 2: The Unregenerate Relationship
Human Spirit Separated from God
and Joined to Sin

Fulfilling the demands of the old master offers no lasting comfort or rest for the unregenerate man, because joy and peace cannot develop from a continuing relationship with sin. The union between the old man of our human spirits and the old master of indwelling sin could promise only eventual ruin. This essentially organic relationship had to be broken. One of the parties had to die. To free us from the bondage of sin, our old man had to be crucified. But we cannot crucify him on our own.

WHO IS THE LIBERATOR?

Now we see the beauty of this phrase "I am [have been] crucified *with Christ*." Not only did Christ die for our sins (see 1 Cor. 15:3), but Jesus Christ also "died unto sin" (Rom. 6:10) to liberate us from the power of sin.

Let this amazing truth sink in to the depths of your being. In order for Jesus Christ to die unto sin, He had to come into union with sin. This is a stunning prospect. On the day of Christ's crucifixion, the earth was darkened for three hours, beginning at noon. Toward the end of that time, Jesus cried out in the darkness, "My God, my God, why hast thou forsaken me?" (Matt. 27:46). These are strong words. Why did Jesus say this? He cried out because a separation had taken place. Jesus, as God the Son and yet functioning as the Son of man, had been separated from God the Father. Because of His union with our sin in order to liberate us, Jesus had to be separated from the Father.

Physical death would soon follow, but this earlier death, this separation of Jesus from His Father, holds far greater significance than the death of Christ's body. It must, because Jesus said, "It is finished," at a certain point before He died physically. Consideration of this pending separation from His Father

and contact with sin was the reason Jesus ago-
nized in the garden of Gethsemane. He was not
shrinking from the cross, for He had come to
save sinners. His agony was because of the *way*
of the cross and the separation from the Father
it entailed.

Think of it: on the cross Jesus, the perfect,
sinless, spotless Lamb of God, was literally separated from God the Father because He was in
actual union with the filth and wickedness of
your sin and mine—and the sin of the entire
world from first to last—thus making Jesus
the "last Adam" (1 Cor. 15:45). Jesus became
sin for us (see 2 Cor. 5:21) not merely legally
but *actually*. Therefore He was forsaken, separated from God the Father, so that we would
not have to be. But when He cried with a loud
voice, "It is finished," and voluntarily gave up
His Spirit (John 19:30), that union with sin
was broken once and for all! "He died unto
sin *once*" (Rom. 6:10).

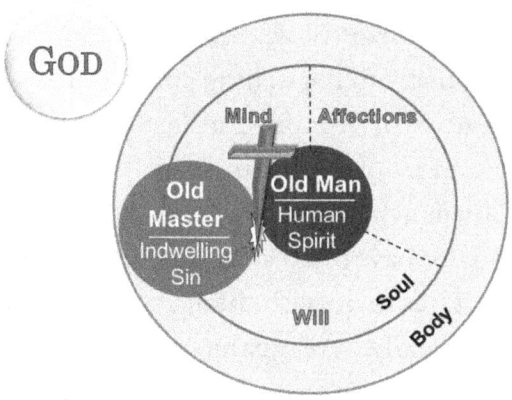

FIGURE 3: Crucified with Christ
Union of Old Master and Old Man Broken

When we believed on Jesus as our Savior, God identified us in Christ and therefore with Christ's history. So at salvation not only did we receive new futures, but we also received new pasts. God identified us in Christ, therefore Christ's history, and therefore His death. The essence of death is separation. At the moment of our salvation, the union of our old man with our old master was forever broken! The cross struck a mortal blow and like a giant knife severed us from indwelling sin. We died to sin (see figure 3). Separated at last! Unshackled! Liberated from indwelling sin!

This is what it means to be "dead to sin." It does not have to do with whether we *feel* dead to sin. It has to do with the *fact* that our human spirits literally were separated from indwelling sin. Our human spirits were forever freed from forced service to the old master of indwelling sin. "He that is dead [who has died] is freed from sin" (Rom. 6:7). Since God identifies us with Christ in Jesus' death to sin, we must embrace this identification as well. Identifying with Christ in this death to sin is a part of the reckoning of Romans 6:11: "Reckon . . . yourselves to be dead indeed unto sin." Reckoning does not create anything; it accounts for the facts accurately.

If a relative died and left you with one million dollars that you then deposited into your account, and if you only put one hundred dollars as the figure in your ledger, you would not be reckoning rightly. As a result, you would live far below your worth. Writing in one million dollars would not create worth; it would account for the worth you already possessed. Similarly, if we do not reckon rightly spiritually, we will live far below our worth in Christ.

Though indwelling sin attempts
to assert its power, sin has mastery
over us no longer—our old master
no longer has authority over us.
The relationship is over!

Remember, it was our old man who died. Our former master of indwelling sin, however, continues to reside in our bodies and souls. In fact, it seeks to operate in our souls and bodies as if it were still in charge.

But though indwelling sin attempts to assert its power, sin has mastery over us no longer—our old master no longer has authority over us. The relationship is over. The old master is no longer *our* master! From this point onward, while we could voluntarily (and foolishly) serve indwelling sin, our days of forced service to sin are forever gone!

At this point you may feel led to shout "Hallelujah!" But wait—from here things get even better.

ALL NEW:
THE PROVISION OF
NEW CREATION

Nevertheless I live; yet not I, but Christ.

GALATIANS 2:20

The second part of the text we began to examine in the previous chapter takes us from crucifixion to resurrection: "I am crucified with Christ; *nevertheless I live; yet not I, but Christ*." More specifically, these words take us to the second vein of truth in this verse, which involves creation. The death of the old man that afforded separation from the old master allows for a creative work of God within us.

We must examine several questions that parallel those we covered in the previous chapter, with one additional question, in order to grasp the significance of this truth and understand crucifixion.

WHICH PART OF US WAS RAISED?

Crucifixion with Christ spoke to a separation, or a death. The second thought conveyed in Galatians 2:20 uses the words "I live" to take us in the other direction: toward life. Remember the part of us that was killed? That part is now raised to life! Just as God identifies us with Christ in His death, so too He identifies us with Christ in His resurrection. God has "raised us up together . . . in Christ" (Eph. 2:6). The old man died with Christ and has now been raised with Christ as the new man (see Col. 3:9–10). This new man is the regenerated human spirit (see figure 4).

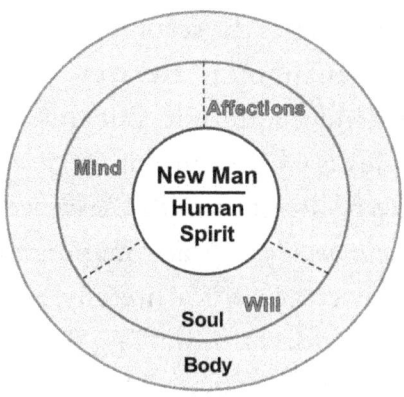

FIGURE 4: Regenerated Man
Spirit (New Man), Soul, and Body

Jesus took all that is of Adam—from the first Adam to the last human being who will ever live—to the cross, which made Him "the last Adam." Then Jesus, as "the second man" (not the second Adam), established a new race (1 Cor. 15:45-47). Since God identifies us with Christ not only in His death to sin but also in His resurrection to life, we too must embrace this identification. Identifying with Christ in this resurrection is the second part of the reckoning of Romans 6:11: "Reckon . . . yourselves to be dead indeed unto sin, but alive unto God through Jesus Christ our Lord."

In this resurrection with Christ, we find the *creation of a new life*: "If any man be in Christ, he is a new creature," or literally, a new "creation" (2 Cor. 5:17), indicating that a creative act of God has taken place. This new creation is described as the "seed" (Greek *sperma*) of God (1 John 3:9), revealing that God implanted in us something of His own nature when we were born again. This is why we are a part of a new race begun by "the second man." God's nature is holy, righteous, loving, and good. This divine nature exists in us right now and has existed in us since the day we were saved. It was in us even on our worst days, when we ignored it. But it was there. With this new creation having taken place, God's love and holiness—His actual life—is now in us. Each of us is now the "new man, which after God is created in righteousness and true holiness" (Eph. 4:24). We "have put on the new man, which is renewed in knowledge after the image of him that created him" (Col. 3:10).

The creation of new life at our core creates a new person—*the real us*. When God created this new life in us, old things passed away, and "all things" became new (2 Cor. 5:17). So what's new? More specifically, what's *all* new? Not our bodies. They're getting older by the day. Though they will be glorified and made new, that prospect is yet future. Not our souls. Though we are being sanctified, at times we think wrongly in our minds, get moody or upset in our emotions, and make wrong choices with our wills. Therefore, the "all new" of 2 Corinthians 5:17 cannot be referring to our body or soul levels. The soul and body are not all new. The only part of us that is all new is our regenerated spirits—our new man.

The creation of new life at our core creates a new person—*the real us*. When God created this new life in us, old things passed away, and "all things" became new.

At salvation we were justified, or declared righteous, even though our souls and bodies are not yet completely righteous. But in our spirits, we are not just declared righteous— we are *actually* righteous. Jesus became sin for us "that we might be made [not just declared] the righteousness of God in him" (2 Cor. 5:21). As Jesus actually (not just legally) became sin for us, we actually (not just legally) are made righteous in Him. Our new man—the real us—is all new!

Amazingly, the Scripture declares that this new part of us, which is God's "seed" making up our regenerated spirits, "cannot sin" (1 John 3:9). Obviously, God's nature cannot sin. This means that we are given sinless provision. It must be so—sinlessness is the nature of God. This is not the same, however, as sinless perfectionism. Experience tells us that we can ignore God's provision and indeed can sin. That is why the Scripture states that *he who abides in Christ* does not sin (see 1 John 3:6). But the point is that the nature of God cannot sin. What an amazing provision! Think of it: our new man is at this very moment righteous and holy. At our core, the real us is comprised of the very nature of God. We are actually righteous—saints, or holy ones.

We often hear of positional truth (Scripture declaring the facts of our standing in Christ) and practical truth (Scripture declaring how we are to act on those facts), but a vital third category exists between these two: provisional truth (Scripture declaring the facts of our sinless provision in Christ). This knowledge bolsters our faith that our behavior can be transformed—that we can see facts turned into function.

So what difference has this creative work made in our mortal bodies? None, as we have noted. They remain as they were. They're not saved and won't be until they're glorified in heaven. So we shouldn't cater to them. Our souls? They're being saved through ongoing, or progressive, sanctification. The progress occurs through faith responses to the Spirit's leadership and power and is greatly hindered through responses of unbelief. But the process continues until we are present with the Lord. What about our spirits? There the creative work is already complete. Our regenerated spirits—the real us—are completely saved. Yes, we can be deceived on the soul level, for "the heart is deceitful above all things, and desperately wicked" (Jer. 17:9). But at our cores, our new man is not desperately wicked; it is radically righteous!

This is the part of us that can grow spiritually. Just as an acorn is perfect as it is yet can grow into a mighty oak tree, so too our new man consisting of God's nature is righteous and holy but can still grow spiritually.

The old master of indwelling sin still hangs around, yet the old man is gone, totally replaced by the new man.

The old man died with Christ and was raised the new man. Therefore, the old man is gone—forever. We cannot have regenerate spirits and unregenerate spirits in the same bodies. The old master of indwelling sin still hangs around, yet the old man is gone, totally replaced by the new man. The new man of our human spirits raised with Christ as a new creation is now actually righteous. As already noted, this must be the case, since the new man consists of God's nature.

But also, with our new man made completely righteous, completely holy, at the point of salvation, this new man is and will remain a fitting habitation for the *Holy* Spirit. There had to be a holy place within us where the Holy Spirit could dwell. Because of this we will see that the creative work of God doesn't end with the introduction of the new man. That new man is brought into a new relationship.

TO WHOM IS OUR NEW MAN JOINED?

The relationship with the old master was broken, and a new relationship was formed (see Rom. 6:15–23). We have a new master! But this new relationship is more than a master-slave association. We were raised with Christ so that we "should be married [joined] to another, even to him who is raised from the dead" (Rom. 7:4). This is the *creation of a new union*, our new man now joined to the risen Christ (see figure 5) through the Holy Spirit. We have, as it were, a new husband.

The Spirit of the resurrected Christ has moved in and joined our regenerated spirits, and "he that is joined unto the Lord is one spirit" (1 Cor. 6:17). Formerly we were dead to God and alive to indwelling sin, separated from God and joined to indwelling sin. Now we are dead to indwelling sin and alive to God, separated from indwelling sin and actually joined to the indwelling Christ. Therefore, our old relationship with indwelling sin is forever severed, and our new relationship with the indwelling Christ is forever sealed! You might feel led again to go ahead and shout "Hallelujah!"

FIGURE 5: Regenerated Relationship
New Man and Holy Spirit (New Master)

WHO IS THE LIBERATOR?

By now the identity of our liberator should be even more obvious: the liberator's name is Jesus—from start to finish! Consider how we came into this glorious liberty: that which set us free from the old master of sin was not a set of intellectually held doctrines; neither was liberation accomplished on our part through actions or exertions in some charitable undertaking. Liberty was gifted to us by the liberator, Jesus, and we received it by faith.

Being set free by Jesus Christ, we can consider now the implications for our liberty, our Christian lives. As we found freedom in neither a set of doctrines nor an assortment of works, our Christian lives are in fact separate from these things as well. They have to be. The Christian life is not a set of doctrines or moral actions. As we noted earlier, many unsaved moralists immerse themselves in works and multiplied teachings. These things are the very fabric of their lives, but the unbelieving know nothing of separation from sin. We, on the other hand, have been loosed from sin's bondage. Because of Jesus liberating us from indwelling sin and joining us in our spirits, our lives are composed of something far better than what our old man offered. The Christian life is a life, a person—His name is Jesus. Jesus Christ Himself is *the Christian life*.

The Christian life is a life, a person—
His name is Jesus. Jesus Christ Himself
is *the Christian life*.

We cannot truly live a Christian life without accessing *the Christian life*. Apart from Jesus, it is impossible to experience true holiness and freedom from sin, because only Christ is able to live a life that always pleases the Father. Only God meets the standard of God. That is why we need Christ's imputed righteousness in justification and His imparted righteousness in sanctification. Thankfully, when we were born again, Christ, the Christian life, moved into us to impart His very life to us so we could live; yet not us but Christ in us—the Christian life. This is not our best for Christ but His best in us—a quality radically different. What an amazing plan of God!

Think of it: a new man who is filled with God's nature and is thus holy and a new master who is the Holy One Himself—is this not a sinless provision? It must be, for God's nature implanted in us is sinless, and the Holy Spirit is sinless. Understand, again, that this is not sinless-perfection teaching but the teaching of sinless *provision*. Sadly, we do not always access our provision in Christ. So there is a difference between sinless provision and sinless perfection.

We have the provision of Jesus: both His nature and His Spirit in us. With this provision we have power for living. In the strictest sense, this living is not a matter of imitation, for humanity cannot imitate deity. This is a matter of *impartation*. The Spirit imparts to us the life of Christ, which allows for us to participate with Him as we become "partakers of the divine nature" (2 Pet. 1:4). This is the Spirit-filled life, the Spirit filling us with the life of Jesus Christ and working in and effecting change in our souls and bodies (see figure 6). Simply put, this is *the Christ life—experiencing Jesus*!

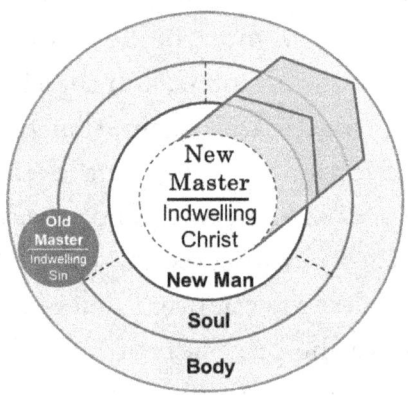

FIGURE 6: Overcoming Life
Imparted Life Filling Spirit, Soul, and Body

ARE THE BENEFITS OF PROVISION AUTOMATIC?

As long as we access the indwelling Christ, we access the freedom from indwelling sin that He won at the cross. But accessing His life is not automatic; it requires a choice on our parts.

The old master of indwelling sin still seeks to operate within our body and soul levels, trying to usurp the place of authority that is no longer his. While he is our *old* master, not our current master, his deceptions suggest that he is presently and assuredly enthroned in our lives. His insistent calls for attention and obedience are known to every believer. Set against this urging to sin is the One who actually is our present master. But our new master does not use the tactics of forced obedience. Rather, He desires a love relationship in which we voluntarily choose Him. Therefore, the indwelling Christ gently leads us to trust Him, to follow Him in paths of righteousness.

So there is a battle with which we are all familiar. The flesh—the place where indwelling sin seeks to operate—lusts, or yearns, against the Spirit, and the Spirit yearns against the flesh (see Gal. 5:17). This is where we make a choice (see figure 7) that leads to ascendancy of either the old master or the new master, leaves us as either carnal or spiritual believers (flesh-filled or Spirit-filled) as evidenced by the works of the flesh or the fruit of the Spirit (see Gal. 5:19–23), and produces either bondage or freedom. We must choose to "walk not after the flesh, but after the Spirit" (Rom. 8:4). We must focus on our real leader—the One with whom we have a relationship of love and faith.

If we walk after the flesh by yielding to indwelling sin, we experience bondage—bondage that we have actually been freed from. How sad and needless! For that defeat does not come from the real us. This is why Paul could say when he sinned, "It is no more I that do it, but sin" (Rom. 7:17). Paul named the culprit: indwelling sin. When we yield to our flesh, we assume responsibility for a sin, but the involved party is not the real us. The

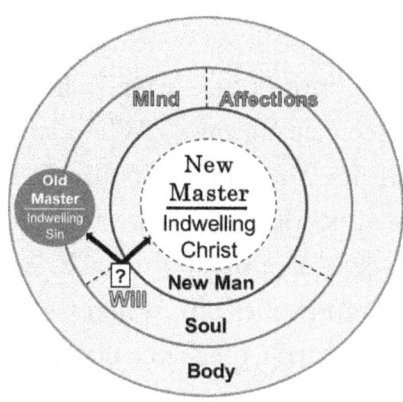

FIGURE 7: Yielding the Will
Choice Determines the Believer's Experience

new man, genuinely holy and righteous and joined unto the Lord—that new creation is the real us. When we commit sin, however, our real us is commandeered by the flesh. It is a tragic identity theft. As a result, "not I but sin" supplies a troublesome false experience; but because of our choice to disobey God, sin becomes our conscious experience, and we experience defeat.

Far better is it to yield to the Spirit and experience "not I but Christ," which is a truth experience (see figure 8). When we make the right choice and allow His life to reign, the battle seems not like a battle at all, for we find the power of the indwelling Christ to be far greater than that of sin. When we yield to the Spirit, the truth experience becomes our conscious experience, and we experience victory. Through faith in the words of God, the Spirit lifts our spirits to rule over soul and body, and thus the Word divides between soul and spirit (see Heb. 4:12).

Perhaps you have heard the following illustration that has been so often used to picture the battle between flesh and Spirit. The scene depicts two dogs fighting inside us, and the one we feed and favor the most wins. This illustration is helpful, in part, because the concept of choosing one to feed and favor reflects the fact that we do make choices that make a real

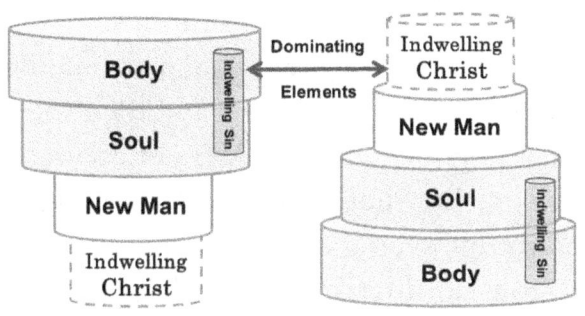

FIGURE 8: Extension of Circle Diagram Sections
Carnal and Spiritual Christians—
Sin or Spirit Mastery

Choosing to yield to the old master, the carnal
Christian, on the left, elevates the flesh and is
dominated by indwelling sin. The spiritual Christian,
on the right, elevates the spirit—the new man
in union with the indwelling Holy Spirit, thereby
keeping the flesh in subjection.

difference. But there is a misleading element
in this illustration that can be rather harmful.
Do we not in our mind's eye picture two dogs

of the same size? I can picture what mine look like—they are *both* big and strong; but equating size with strength and then thinking of dogs of equal size does not accurately depict reality—not even close. Indwelling sin and the indwelling Christ are far from equals in strength. Matching a small Chihuahua against a Rottweiler or a Doberman would still fail to provide an accurate picture. The difference is far greater than any such illustration can portray.

So as for the combatants, yes, we have the flesh, where indwelling sin seeks to deceive. More importantly, there stands against the flesh one Spirit: our spirit now comprised of God's divine nature righteous and holy in union with the Holy Spirit of the enthroned Christ, who sits "far above all principality, and power" (Eph. 1:20-21). Jesus is victory—the victorious life Himself. When we access this phenomenal provision, we win the battle. It is nothing for the indwelling Christ to conquer the Chihuahua of the flesh!

Jesus is victory—the victorious life Himself. When we access this phenomenal provision, we win the battle.

Understanding the ease with which the Lord conquers, we should consider next what such conquering looks like.

3

POWER MOVES:
THE LAW OF
COUNTERACTION

Christy liveth in me.

GALATIANS 2:20

The third vein of truth in this goldmine text is highlighted by the phrase "Christ liveth [lives] in me." When by faith we access the life of Christ *living* in us, Christ conquers fleshly desire. Christ is the overcoming life Himself. His very life overcomes, or *counteracts*, our flesh. Authors of some of the classic Christian works from generations past referred to this spiritual dynamic as the *principle of counteraction*. It is the means of victory.

We need a deeper understanding of this principle, but to better frame the concept, it will be helpful to address first some common misunderstandings in regard to living a life of victory. Let's clear out wrong ideas and replace them with the right idea.

WRONG IDEAS

One can find quite a few wrong ideas among professing believers about how to attain victory in our spiritual lives. We will examine three categories and show how each one misses the mark.

Struggle Theology

One category of wrong ideas contains the various deceptions of "struggle theology."

Obviously, this side of heaven we all experience various struggles in the sense that we all face trials. But the struggle of attempting to live the Christ life without accessing the life of Christ does not need to be one of them.

Victory is not achieved by *trying harder*. Reliance on self-effort is a common mistake that believers make. Many embrace justification by faith but then regress to thinking of sanctification by works. Saved by faith and then self-dependent for victorious living? It's been attempted and proven not to work. The apostle Paul dedicated the seventh chapter of Romans to describing the frustration and futility of trying to keep the law without the power of the Holy Spirit. Flesh dependence simply cannot overcome flesh dominance. We can try all we want, but in the end, the enemy cannot be counted on to defeat the enemy. We began in the Spirit by faith, and we must continue in the Spirit by faith (see Gal. 3:1–3).

> Victory is not achieved by
> *trying harder*. It's been attempted
> and proven not to work.

Still, the devil seeks to deceive Christians into attempting to live the Christian life without the life of Christ. The devil wants us to think that when we fail, redoubled efforts with greater grit and determination will bring success. It's not true. Trying harder leads only to further defeat—either the obvious defeat of flesh indulgence or the subtle defeat of flesh dependence. The former is giving in to unrighteousness—the *works* of the flesh; the latter is catering to self-righteousness—the *work* of the flesh. The former is irreligion; the latter is counterfeit religion. Jesus insisted that the flesh profits nothing (see John 6:63) and that apart from Him we can do nothing (see John 15:5). Satan does not care which avenue of the flesh we take as long as it's on the flesh that we place our hopes. He knows that no matter how hard we try to live as we should, as long as our efforts are just in our flesh, they amount to nothing that really counts.

Victory is not gained through *accessing the right power while having the wrong goal*. Some awaken to the power of Jesus but still have a goal other than Jesus—generally their own moral or spiritual standards. But victory is not through our supposed dependence on the power of the Spirit to maintain our own versions of what Christianity should look like. The problem with this model is that it is essentially a law focus—and this does not lead to victory, even if our own ideas of what Christianity should look like involve good things. It's supposed dependence on the right power but with a wrong goal. The goal is something other than Jesus—as if that's better than Jesus.

Whatever we focus on we depend on. We are to be "looking unto Jesus [our focus] the author and finisher of our faith [on whom we depend]" (Heb. 12:2). So if we focus on the law or our version of law keeping as our goal, we end up depending on the law, which is ultimately flesh dependence. Those in this deception are not depending on the power of the Spirit as much as they think they are. This is the real dilemma of the frustration and defeat of Romans 7. But Jesus is not only the source of life; He is the goal of life. When He is our goal, we depend on Him. When we depend on Him, He lives through us—and our Christianity looks right, wherever we are on our journeys with Him.

This is not standards bashing; it is confronting the error of standards focus and standards dependence. Spirituality is not developed through keeping certain lifestyle rituals. Unsaved moralists can do that. Spirituality is developed through being rightly related to the Spirit. When we walk in the Spirit, we evidence the fruit of the Spirit. This is true holiness. As we focus on Christ as our leader—when we make Him our goal—He will lead us to whatever standards He knows we need, but our dependence will be on Him, not our standards.

Spirituality is not developed through keeping rituals but through being rightly related to the Spirit.

Victory is not achieved by *a diligent watchfulness against sinning.* This method sounds correct, but again, its focus is wrong. Reliance on one's own watchfulness amounts to a subtle form of self-dependence. In this deception the focus is again on an individual's holiness instead of on the holy One. Those snared in this trap can become anxious and joyless, and in spite of their purported watchfulness, their focus on personal holiness facilitates the obvious sin of pride. At the least, this focus incorporates a split focus between Christ and standards (diligent watchfulness against sinning). But a split trust reveals mistrust in Christ alone. In the matter of justification, people miss heaven for this error. Therefore, in the matter of sanctification, this is no small matter.

Our focus reveals our dependence. God dependence presupposes God focus. While it is vital that each believer apply the standards that the Holy Spirit leads each of us to apply, our focus must ever be on the holy One, not on holiness. The Holy Spirit does lead us to lifestyle applications, and when He does, we must obey. But when our focus is right, our dependence will be on the Holy Spirit, not the applications.

Victory is not through *suppression of sin*. Similar to the ones trying harder are those who think they can suppress the draw of indwelling sin in their flesh. For example, when confronted with a provoking situation, a deceived believer may think he is victorious because he refrained from lashing out at the one causing him trouble, even though inside he was seething. But such a hollow triumph is hardly victory. The efforts that produce an outward appearance of control do nothing to suppress the inward desire to see an adversary brought down and a score settled. True victory yields peace, because it removes our desire for self-justification. Such peace is a quality that suppression cannot deliver.

Victory is not through *service-oriented sanctification*. Some think they can stand triumphant if they are just diligent enough in service. Those who believe this are of a kindred spirit with those insisting on trying harder. Active and driven, such people often display a spirit of volunteerism that seems commendable, but the motive behind their actions is not right. While it is true that there is no true sanctification without service, Scripture clearly maintains that service is not the source of sanctifying influence.

"Do Nothing" Deceptions

A second category of wrong ideas contains the "do nothing" deceptions. This is the opposite of struggle theology and consists of putting forth little to no effort to gain victory in our walk with Christ.

A deceived believer may think he is victorious because he refrained from lashing out at the one causing him trouble while inside he was seething. But such a hollow triumph is hardly victory.

Victory is not through *passivity*. Though sitting back in a somewhat paralyzed condition strikes some as victory in the name of faith, such passivity is no more than *easy-believism* regarding sanctification. As we saw earlier, faith is not a work but dependence on the worker—Jesus—and this demands of us an active trust in God *to work*. Therefore, although our victory is not gained through the self-effort of trying harder, victory does come through trusting God to work. Victory without trying is not victory by doing nothing; it is victory through trusting. It is not a matter of "just obey" (trying harder), nor is it a matter of "just trust" (passivity); it is a matter of "trust to obey."

Victory is not by *an inevitable matter of course*. Some count on sanctification inevitably taking place as a matter of God's sovereignty. Obviously, God is sovereign, but in His sovereignty God makes man responsible to walk by faith. Misunderstanding God's sovereignty diminishes God's design for personal responsibility. Fatalistic thinking ignores the sovereign God's hortatory admonitions that we cooperate with Him in faith.

> God is sovereign, but in His sovereignty He makes man responsible to walk by faith.

Victory is not by *inevitable gradual growth.* Similar to the previous misconception, some think that growth in grace is not only inevitable but of necessity steadily slow, not able to be either hindered or accelerated by the believer in Christ. How depressing! Such thinking pushes Christian victory far out into the future and discourages believers in any definite faith steps toward that end. This deception implies that all new Christians are anemic and insists that the duration of one's life after salvation correlates to how strong one will end up being in the Lord. Practical experience reveals that this is not inevitably the case. The church is filled with examples of converts who have grown in grace relatively quickly as well as longstanding believers who, sadly, still need to be fed with milk instead of meat.

An insistence on gradual inevitable progress confuses growth with maturity. The experience and trials of a believer are key facets of the maturing process, and of necessity these require a longer period before their deep benefits are realized. Growth, however, can be seen in the short term. Growing in grace through walking by faith can and must commence immediately upon the new birth. Brand-new believers can and should be filled with the Spirit. When new believers are Spirit filled, they are "spiritual," that is, they are rightly related to the Spirit even though not necessarily mature. Once started on the path of walking in the Spirit, growth can be stunted through choices of unbelief or accelerated through choices of faith. Given this, growth is not necessarily steady and not always slow. The victory that comes with growing in grace can be possessed in the present. It does not need to be a dim goal that stands apart from us at such a great distance.

Eradication of Sin

Yet there is a third category of wrong thinking.

Victory is not *eradication of indwelling sin*. Some erroneously think that somehow the old master of indwelling sin has been banished from their lives. While at salvation our old man died, the old master still resides in our bodies and souls. Separation from the old master of indwelling sin afforded creation of the new man in us—a sinless provision—but Scripture in no wise indicates that the old master has been expelled and that sinless perfection is a given. Instead, we find that indwelling sin still remains and operates, sometimes quite successfully, through deception on our body and soul levels. Thinking that sin is gone when it is actually present will lead only to defeat.

THE RIGHT IDEA

The principle, or law, of counteraction is simply the truth of a greater law counteracting and overcoming a lesser law. An important positional truth maintains that the law of the Spirit of life in Christ Jesus has made us free from the law of sin and death (see Rom. 8:2). This greater law, the law of the Spirit of life in Christ, liberates, or frees, us from the lesser claim: the law of sin. Note that it does not indicate that the law of sin has been repealed and removed from human experience; rather, it states that a greater law counteracts and overcomes the existing lesser law.

> Through the Spirit we can counteract
> and overcome the pull of old habits.
> Over time we can abandon familiar,
> unprofitable ways, and in their place
> new, good habits can flourish.

Based on this positional truth and the provisional truth of the indwelling Christ in our new man, the facts (positional truth and provisional truth) can be turned into function (practical truth). Scripture claims that if we *through the Spirit* confront the deeds of the body, we shall live (see Rom. 8:13). Through the Spirit we can counteract and overcome the pull of old habits. Over time we can abandon familiar, unprofitable ways, and in their place new, good habits can flourish. In other words, we can exchange bad acquired habits for good acquired habits.

The law of the Spirit of life in Christ frees us from the law of sin. This is the "law of liberty"

(James 1:25). A greater law counteracts and overcomes a lesser law. This is the law of counteraction as the power of the Spirit moves to overcome the power of the flesh.

STAY IN THE BASKET!

Many examples in the physical realm illustrate this concept of counteracting a lesser law. Consider the law of gravity. We are well aware of a downward gravitational pull toward the earth. Throw a rock into the air and gravity will arrest the rock's ascent and bring it back down. But greater laws can counteract and overcome the law of gravity. For instance, because warm air has less mass than an equal volume of cool air, warm air is lighter and experiences less of a gravitational pull, and therefore it rises above heavier, cooler air. Stated in non-scientific terms, this is the law of *warm air rising*.

Hot-air balloons depend on warm air rising to overcome gravity. When a balloon is ready for liftoff, someone releases the tether lines, and the balloon immediately soars skyward. Think of a young student who has just learned about gravity watching a balloon's effortless climb. In amazement she might think, *Wow! Look at that. There is no more law of gravity!* But of course her observation isn't in line with the facts; the law of gravity remains. What she is witnessing is counteraction of gravity by a greater law.

Imagine now that you are about to take a hot-air-balloon ride. When the balloon is ready, you get into the basket. The ropes are released, the balloon ascends, and as the balloon soars skyward, so do you—because you're in the basket. As long as you stay in the basket, you benefit from the dynamics involved as the law of warm air rising counteracts and overcomes the law of gravity.

Now suppose after an hour of thoroughly enjoying the ride and all the views that come with it, you get to thinking, *Wow! Never in my life have I been suspended like this in midair for a solid hour!* One impulsive thought later, you conclude, *You know, I don't think the law of gravity has any more power over me!* Recklessly emboldened, you take one courageous step and find yourself out of the basket—falling. As you plummet toward earth, it hits you: the law of gravity is still there, and, importantly, it still has power over you. So what's the key to keeping safe and preventing the law of gravity from exerting its power over you? It's fairly simple: *stay in the basket!* Keep depending on the basket. Keep *abiding* in the basket. For every moment—not just at some points or even for most of the time—but literally for every moment you stay in the basket, you experience the lift that comes from the law of warm air rising counteracting and delivering you from the power of the law of gravity.

What's the key to keeping safe and preventing the law of gravity from exerting its power over you?
It's fairly simple: *stay in the basket!*

Let's make the analogy, and I hope you're ahead of me. The law of sin is like the law of gravity—the constant downward pull we all experience every day. But the law of the Spirit is like the law of warm air rising, the greater law. In our illustration the basket is Christ. Note that the law of the Spirit is the law of the Spirit of life *in Christ*. Jesus commands us, "Abide in me" (John 15:4). For the sake of our illustration, the command could be rendered, "Stay in the basket." Why? Because when we abide in Christ by staying in the basket, we access the spiritual dynamics involved. The law of the Spirit of life in Christ counteracts and overcomes the law of sin just as the law of warm air rising counteracts and overcomes the law of gravity.

If you have been saved for any length of time, then undoubtedly you have experienced the principle of counteraction whether you understood this truth or not. Have you ever noticed that when some people trust Christ as Savior, certain sinful habits fall away from them immediately? Why? The change appears automatic, but it's not. As we have noted, in order to get saved, one must look unto Jesus. This is faith. Some new believers just keep looking unto Jesus. They stay in the basket. As they trust in Christ, they access the life of Christ—and He does not have any sinful habits. That's why old things can fall away from them so quickly. The key is abiding, staying in the basket. If at some point they stop looking to Jesus and step out of the basket, the pull of that ever-present law of sin is ready to reclaim them, and down they go.

Yet even when we find ourselves in what is sometimes called a wilderness wandering, are there not times when we get so desperate that we accidentally happen into faith? Compelled by that desperation, we cry out to God for deliverance. That is faith. That is getting into the basket. We experience a supernatural lift, but when the crisis is past, our dependence on God fades, and from the safety of the basket, we take that step out—and down. This phenomenon often leaves people puzzled. The common experience of regular defeat is surprisingly interrupted by sudden fleeting victory, and because the principle of abiding is strangely foreign to many of us, it proves difficult to comprehend why we realized even such a small measure of victory.

When we understand the spiritual dynamics involved, we know that the way into the basket is also the means of staying in the basket: making choices of faith. Not staying in the basket is not exercising faith. At this point, it is important to note that a failure to exercise faith does not suggest a loss of salvation. To be saved is to receive eternal life. And by definition, we cannot have *eternal* life for just a little while. Exiting the basket simply means not accessing the abundant life available to us through abiding in Christ. It's forfeiting victory. So *stay in the basket!*

When we stay in the basket, we grow in grace through our walk of faith and experience the abundant, uplifting life of Christ. Others will see it too. That most cantankerous Christian J. Elder Cumming shed his natural belligerence and radiated the life and love of Christ. So can we. Cumming moved forward into a joyous life of regular victory punctuated by surprising instances of defeat. So can we. This is the essence of personal revival, being restored to spiritual life—the life of Christ. It is the eternal life of Christ accessed as the abundant life of Christ.

> When we stay in the basket,
> we grow in grace through our walk of
> faith and experience the abundant,
> uplifting life of Christ. This is the
> essence of personal revival.

In revival we will not only be cleansed through the blood of Jesus, but we will also experience victory we didn't think possible this side of heaven. Many have testified to this reality. But with this experience, we must take care to remember from whence it came. We could fall into thinking that experiencing so much new victory has insulated us from the law of sin. If we believe for a moment that the law of sin has no continuing power over us, then we will find that we have just stepped out of the basket. Our inevitable plummet should serve to remind us that the law of sin, like gravity, still waits to exhibit power over those who stray from the safety of a greater power.

By the way, the higher we soar, the farther we have to fall. So what's the key? *Stay in the basket!* Keep depending on Christ. Keep *abiding* in Christ. Every moment we abide in Christ, not just some or most, we will experience His lifting life of victory.

AN EXPERIENCE IN COUNTERACTION

Interestingly, when I first started using this basket illustration in 1999, my wife remarked, "If you ever go on a hot-air-balloon ride, you will be going by yourself!" Not too many months later, my home church in Ann Arbor, Michigan, decided to surprise my wife and me with—you guessed it—a hot-air-balloon ride. Since it was a special surprise and because much of the church planned to attend the launch, my wife dutifully went along with it (and ended up enjoying it too). When we arrived at the scene, the balloon was lying flat on the ground, spread out and ready. After a check of wind currents and other details, the time soon came to introduce the element that on our behalf would overcome the restrictive pull of gravity: hot air filled the balloon.

With the filling process complete, we were instructed to enter the basket. Five of us were to ride that day. Besides my wife and me, there were the pastor of the church, his wife (my sister), and, of course, the pilot. Each of us stepped in. After giving a few words of instruction, the pilot smiled at us and asked, "Are you ready?" We all smiled and, in spite of how we truly may have felt, found ourselves answering, "Yes!" The pilot reached out and unclipped the lone rope that bound us to our familiar plane. With an audible *whoosh*, the balloon immediately soared upward. It seemed as if we were a hundred feet in the air within seconds. One thing was quite evident: we were rising quickly by a power not our own.

As we enjoyed the ride that day, we experienced no struggle. We went with the wind. If only we as believers would walk in like manner with the wind of the Spirit, it would keep us from so much unnecessary struggle. As the five of us appreciated the beauty of the scenes below, we also understood the value of what proved to be an amazingly easy choice: our collective decision to stay in the basket! If only we as believers in Christ would understand the reality of the spiritual dynamics illustrated by the basket and choosing to abide, the impact would make our Christian walks so much easier.

Counteraction is not a matter of the Spirit enabling our flesh to do right. It is a matter of depending on the Spirit.

Counteraction. This is not a matter of the Spirit enabling our flesh to do right. The flesh never does right. The flesh never improves. In fact, the flesh can only grow worse. Counteraction is a matter of depending on the Spirit. Also, this matter has nothing to do with the Spirit's power combining with our strength. At the inception of our spiritual lives, depending to any degree on our own contributions in combination with the work of the cross would keep us from salvation. Remember, a split trust falls short of faith in Christ alone. The same holds true with sanctification and service. There's no combining our strength with His. Spiritual ministry demands spiritual energy.

You and I are weak apart from Christ and will always be this side of heaven. The Spirit-filled life is not us becoming strong and dedicating our strength to God's cause. Rather, the Spirit-filled life is a matter of us recognizing our weakness so that we continually depend on the strong one: Jesus. This is staying in the basket! But if staying where we should is not automatic and not dependent on personal effort, then how is it accomplished? It demands the cooperation of faith.

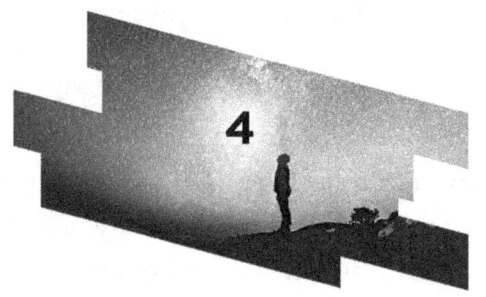

SIMPLE FAITH:
THE RESPONSIBILITY
OF COOPERATION

*The life which I now live in the flesh
I live by the faith of the Son of God, who
loved me, and gave himself for me.*

GALATIANS 2:20

We come now to our final examination of this magnificent text: "The life which I now live in the flesh [the mortal body] I live by the faith of [by faith in] the

97

Son of God, who loved me, and gave himself for me." The fourth vein of truth in this verse can be articulated in the words "The life which I now live . . . I live by . . . faith." Forget trying harder and struggling to do better. No work of our own will win us victory. Abandon the idle waiting of passivity, and note the critical emphasis of the passage: we live by the simple cooperation of faith. There's victory.

Properly understood, it is victory *with trusting*. The cooperation of faith is a matter of trusting the Lord for obedience. We trust to obey. Faith is not a work but rather dependence on the worker—Jesus. This cooperation is easily divided into three faith steps.

REJECT ANY LIES

Before we take the provision of the Christ life, we may need to reject any lies the adversary of our souls has offered us about ourselves and about God.

Satan whispers many *lies about each of us*. Have you bought into those lies?

You may think you're a failure and a loser, that you're forever defined by the shame and guilt you feel from your worst day—whether from some stumbling you now greatly regret or abuse you sadly suffered. But these thoughts of failure are all a lie. In Christ we are winners because He won for us and lives in us, and God defines us by who we are in Christ—as *righteous*—even though at times we may stumble and fail.

You may think you'll never measure up. But in Christ each of us already measures up, because He measured up for us. The father of lies tells us that we are righteous only legally but not actually. But the truth is that at our cores, the real us is actually righteous. The accuser claims that we'll never get better this

side of heaven in order to make us preoccu-
pied with our next failure. But the Word of
God says that we are righteous and have the
privilege of maturing into what we already are,
so by embracing the truth we can get excited
about our next victory in Christ.

The accuser claims that we'll never get
better this side of heaven.
But the Word of God says that we are
righteous and have the privilege of
maturing into what we already are.

You may think you're a failure, so you
might as well enjoy sin. But God says that we
are righteous, so we might as well enjoy righteousness. The lie claims that we're just saved
sinners. The truth claims that we're saints who
still sin—a radically different focus from that
of the lie. The lie causes us to fixate on the

idea that we are fundamentally flawed. But the truth resounds with the reality that based on our identification with Christ, we are fundamentally fixed!

Reject any lies about yourself.

Satan also whispers *lies about God.* Have you bought into those lies?

The lie says that God cannot satisfy us as much as some sin can. But the truth is, only Jesus satisfies. This is made obvious by the bondage that sinful choices bring versus the liberty that yielding to Christ brings.

The lie claims that God loves us less when we sin and more when we don't. If you have bought into this lie, you have a performance-based grid of sanctification. You are in the Galatian error. But the truth is that God loves us unconditionally—as much on our worst day as on our best. Let that truth sink in! Obviously God never condones sin. Our sin choices grieve the Spirit (see Eph. 4:30). But only one who truly loves us can be truly grieved over our sin. Understanding all this does not repel us from Christ but rather attracts us to Him.

The lie states that God is distant from us when we sin, that He is angry and disgusted with us. But the truth is that although sin causes distance between us and God's blessings, we and God are joined, and He lovingly seeks to bring us back to a place of implicit trust in Him for cleansing and freedom.

Reject any lies about God.

Satan also whispers *lies about our real response*—the response of the real us (the new man) to the real leader (the indwelling Christ). Ultimately, we may think that we want sin. But that's a lie! The real us, the new man, wants the real leader, the new master—every time. We may ask, "Then why does it feel like I want sin?" Because the old master of indwelling sin who still seeks to operate in our flesh seeks to deceive us into thinking that he's us and we're him. But we're not him, and he's not us! The "bad wants" are the desires of the flesh—not us. The "oughts" are really the "wants" of the real us. The new man composed of God's nature wants what Jesus wants every time.

> We must reject the lies and take our provision in Christ—and the draw toward sin will immediately subside.

Temptation itself is not sin. Jesus said to pray lest we enter into temptation (see Luke 22:46). Therefore, temptation is not sin—entering into temptation is. When we enter into temptation, we need to confess our wrong choices and trust in Christ's blood to cleanse us (see 1 John 1:9). But if we have not entered into the temptation, we do not need to confess—we need to reject. When a snare in the world system triggers some temptation that we feel drawn to in our flesh, that pull is not the real us; it's indwelling sin seeking to deceive us. When a fiery dart hits us seemingly out of nowhere, launching sinful thoughts or producing dark feelings, that's not us; it's the enemy tempting us. Remember, the temptation itself is not sin. We must reject the lies and take our provision in Christ—and the draw toward sin will immediately subside.

TAKE THE PROVISION

The Scripture says that faith comes "by hearing, and hearing by the word of God" (Rom. 10:17). In the English translation of the Greek New Testament, the term "word" is from either *logos* or *rhema*. *Logos* generally refers to the whole of God's Word, the Bible, while *rhema* points to specific statements (specific words) contained within the *logos*. Because "word" in Romans 10:17 is translated from *rhema*, we understand that faith is sourced from particular statements of Scripture.

Our text, Galatians 2:20, is one such *rhema*, or word, of God, and the faith-nourishing fact presented here is our provision for victory: Christ lives in you and me. Note that the tense of the verb the apostle used to describe Christ's living does not make this a future promise. Paul used a present tense, indicating a present fact: *Christ is living in me.* As children of God, Christ is living in each of us right now.

If we place this glorious fact alongside a recent defeat we have experienced, examining our actions may lead to confusion. "Christ living in me? Right now? Then how could I have blown it so badly today?" Keep in mind the key to counteraction: it is paramount that we stay in the basket. The specific word of our text insists that living is to be by *faith*. Faith turns what is true provisionally into experience practically. We simply must choose to depend on the reality of the words declared by God in order to access the benefit of what God says is so. In this case, our specific word of God is stated as a fact and not a conditional promise. Therefore, we do not need to ask Christ to live in us or beg Him to return to us. He is in us—living in us right now. We just need to *take* God at His word.

Taking God at His word implies that we
are taking what God is giving—
Christ's life in us. It's as simple as taking
a gift from someone who
offers it to us and saying thank you.

Taking God at His word implies that we are taking what God is giving—Christ's life in us: "Thanks be to God, which giveth [who gives] us the victory through our Lord Jesus

Christ" (1 Cor. 15:57). Since God gives us the victory—Jesus Christ—then we must take hold of the life of Christ living in us. It's as simple as taking a gift from someone who offers it to us and saying thank you. It's that real! While what we are talking about is spiritual, not physical, it's just as real as if it were a material gift. So take the victorious life Himself—Jesus—and then say thank You!

Christ is living in us! By faith we must take that reality as we face situations that need the supernatural lift of the Spirit. This is walking by faith. This is walking in the Spirit, through whom we overcome the desires of the flesh (see Gal. 5:16). Through this means we do not fulfill fleshly desires. This is abiding in Christ. This is staying in the basket! We must take the reality of Christ living in us and say thank You! It really is that real. The "thank You!" means that we believe we have received the gift and now may act on it.

ACT ON IT

Once we have taken the provision of victory, we must act on it, simply trusting in the reality of the words of God regardless of how we feel. This is trusting to obey. Do not misinterpret this as resolving to *just obey* or *just act*, for that would be self-dependent action. Also avoid thinking of it as needing to *just trust*, for such passivity is not really trusting. As the song says, victory is a matter of "Trust *and* Obey," or, as we have stated it, *trust to obey*. Trusting (taking the provision) accesses the life of Christ living in us so that when we obey (act on that provision), the law of the Spirit enables us to follow through with the intended steps. Taking our provision in Christ and acting on it is God-dependent, Spirit-enabled obedience. In doing this, we experience Christ as our life, and our actions always please the Father. This is experiencing Jesus.

Faith is always a response to the Spirit's convincing work in our life to trust and obey (see Phil. 2:13). So we must cooperate with Him. But cooperation with the Spirit is not a mechanical application of the steps of faith. This is where most people fail. *The key is relationship, not ritual.* If we do not value our relationship with Jesus, we will find ourselves not wanting to take the faith steps but instead, out of duty, merely going through the motions. This is a deception, since it is not real faith. But when we focus on Jesus, enjoying Him and valuing our relationship with Him through the Spirit, we will truly desire to cooperate with Him by faith. We need to focus on Jesus—the provider—through His nature in us and His Spirit in us. When the stuff of life confronts us and victory seems impossible—and it is without Jesus—know that faith is not a work. It is dependence on the worker—Jesus, the One who never fails. His life wins, including His life in us when we access it by simple faith.

A number of years ago I realized that I had allowed myself to become quite bitter and unwilling to forgive someone for a particular wrong. But through the gracious working of the Spirit, after confessing my bitterness to God and taking His cleansing, I said to Him, "Lord, I do not feel anything, but by Your grace, I forgive so and so." God freed me and began a reviving process in my life. "By Your grace"—that was the *taking*. Concluding the transaction with "I forgive"—that was the *acting*. We show trust when we take what God is providing, convinced that it is sufficient for our present need, and then act on it in the confidence of that sufficiency.

Jesus Christ is sufficient.
He lives in us to impart to us
His victorious life.

How many men are confronted almost daily with the temptation to think impurely because of the immodesty and sensuality that pervade our society? Can anyone stand victorious before that onslaught? Thankfully, Jesus Christ is sufficient. He could live unscathed in our society, and He lives in us to impart to us His victorious life. When we are tempted to think wrongly, we need to bear in mind that the temptation itself is not sin. We can just say, "Thank You, Lord, for Your life." That is taking the provision of Christ living in us. Then in faith, we can look the other way. That is acting on it. As we do this, the Spirit enables us to look away and be free from what we saw—as if we never saw it. This is not the same as a self-dependent striving in which powerless flesh-dependence tries to overcome flesh-indulgence. In that scenario, it's flesh pitted against flesh in a struggle doomed from the start. It is merely striving as we turn our heads the other way but our hearts remain fixed on the temptation. In contrast, taking hold of Jesus to enable us to look the other way accesses for us the liberating deliverance of the life of Christ in us.

A friend of mine once told me of a visit to a shopping mall he had made with some friends. Though the atmosphere of the typical mall hardly lends itself to spirituality (and this one was no exception), he stayed in the basket, and the Spirit enabled him to keep taking hold of grace. Taking and acting, trusting to obey, enjoying the freedom that is in Christ, my friend testified that he emerged from the mall victorious, unspotted by the world. It was as if he had not gone through the mall at all.

Perhaps you have an anger problem. You may be easily provoked. Help is at hand. I once met such a man while preaching at his church, and he told me that he had been a terrible testimony in his workplace. He pointed out that after hearing the truth of Galatians 2:20, he just kept reminding himself throughout the next day to "stay in the basket!" On the final night of a week of meetings, he shared a story with me: "Today at work we had a staff meeting. I knew it had the potential to be a provoking session. But I wanted to see God change me." He then held up a small object and continued, "To help me remember to trust Christ, I brought this little basket to the table to remind me to *stay in the basket*!" With the joy of the Lord radiating from his face, he testified to victory in Christ.

Perhaps for you it is not so much showing outward anger as it is becoming irritable and impatient. While preaching in another church, a young mother of several children came to me after a service. She held one child in her arms as the others stood close by. Seemingly exasperated, she asked me, "How do I apply this, for example, when I follow the kids into the bathroom at home and discover that they've just messed up everything? You can imagine my frustration. How does it work?" Reminding her once more of the provision of Christ actually living in her, I said that in the moment of provocation, she simply must take Christ's life and say thank You, presently trusting Him to impart His patience so she could respond with His grace. Take and act. Trust to obey. Just then one of her little girls went over to a table in the church lobby. She grabbed a jar filled with small objects and decided it would be fun to dump the contents onto the floor. As this mother looked over at the mess, she realized she was in a real-life testing—and she burst out in laughter. She took the provision in that provoking moment, and irritation was nowhere to be found. That's how it works!

In the basket is blessed victory.
Reject any lies, take the provision,
act on it—and experience Jesus!

The Lord expects each of us to experience His victory, and He has placed the power that is His life easily within our reach. You and I are personally responsible for staying in the basket. Then, once in, our words and transformed lives should encourage others to enter in as well. It should go without saying, however, that our exhortations to others to abide in Christ carry more weight when we offer them from within the security of the basket.

A man once told me of a tiff he'd had with his wife during a week of meetings that I had held at his church. Remembering something of the preaching, his wife took exception with him, exclaiming, "You were out of the basket!" With a glint in his eye, he replied, "Well, you're out of the basket yourself for telling me that I'm out of it!" Doubtless each of their observations bore the stamp of truth. However, while we can appreciate the humor in the retelling of such an exchange, we must remember that our primary responsibility is not to stand by and speak of someone else being in or out of the basket. We need to maintain a singular focus on Jesus in order to stay and keep staying in the basket. As we abide in Him, the Spirit will find us to be clear channels by which He can reach believers who are straying from truth and those on the outside who have yet to believe.

On the night following a service at which I had preached the truths of Galatians 2:20, I asked a man, "Did you stay in the basket today?" A little sheepishly he responded, "Well—I got out." Without pausing to elaborate on the failure, his face lifted as he hastened to say, "But I got right back in!" This highlights a great point. Should we step out of the basket, we certainly will experience defeat, but we don't need to wallow in it. Without making excuses, we can get honest with God about exiting and then take hold of the cleansing power of the blood of Jesus (see 1 John 1:9). We can confess the sin, then take hold of a clean heart and thank the Lord for it. This is walking in the light (see 1 John 1:7)—our means of getting back in the basket. Once in, we can again walk in the Spirit, the means whereby we stay in the basket.

In the basket is blessed victory. Reject any lies, take the provision, act on it—and experience Jesus! Experiencing Jesus makes it possible for us to be regularly victorious. Joy is to be our lot, and the startling surprise of a defeat should only drive us back into the familiar safety of our Savior's arms where we can find forgiveness and restoration. The avenue that J. Elder Cumming followed away from being a cantankerous Christian to one filled with the love of God is available to us. We can realize victory through cooperating with the Spirit by faith, experiencing the principle of counteraction, which has its basis in our having been crucified with Christ, His creation of a new life in us, and our union with His life. Simply put, since Christ is living in us, we can live in victory by abiding in Him so that He abides in us. This is the Christ life! This is experiencing Jesus!

Stay in the basket!

NOTE

Introduction: Finding Hope in Rediscovering Christ

1. The story of J. Elder Cumming is found in Steven Barabas, *So Great Salvation: The History and Message of the Keswick Convention* (Eugene, OR: Wipf & Stock, 2005).

Exploring the Glorious Freedom of
Divine Cleansing, Enabling and Authority

The
Revived
Life

JOHN R. VAN GELDEREN
FOREWORD BY RICHARD OWEN ROBERTS

THE REVIVED LIFE

Greater than any craving for food and water is the deep longing within the soul of many of God's children to be like Jesus—to be holy and victorious over evil and loving and effective in service. In a word, to experience Christ's life.

If you've felt these longings but are discouraged and defeated, separated from the life of Christ by the rising waters of failure, the Word of God provides hope and help. Laying down biblical stepping stones, John Van Gelderen leads you on a journey to a life that overcomes sin and overflows into ministry to others.

To order visit www.revivalfocus.org.

THE FAITH RESPONSE

Is faith a work—or is it a gift? What is the role of human responsibility in all this?

In *The Faith Response*, John Van Gelderen addresses this confusion by outlining a proper biblical understanding of the nature of faith, which is true God-dependence—realizing that "I can't, but God can"— and he doesn't stop there. In later chapters he makes practical application of this truth to our daily walk with God, showing how total dependence on God is wrapped up in the secret of "Christ in you, the hope of glory."

To order visit www.revivalfocus.org.

FRIENDSHIP WITH THE HOLY SPIRIT

Many today long for a closer walk with God—a more personal relationship than they have. The Holy Spirit of God makes such a relationship personal and real. Yet the extremes of strange fire and no fire have caused many to miss out on God's plan for this age. *Friendship with the Holy Spirit* shows from the Scriptures how to develop a vibrant and personal relationship with the Spirit of Christ. Truly friendship with the Holy Spirit is the revival relationship!

To order visit www.revivalfocus.org.

THE REVIVAL JOURNEY

The Revival Journey maps out the discernible phases of revival as revealed in Scripture and illustrated by history. As such, it may serve as a practical manual for those seeking to exercise faith for revival. At the same time, it may serve as a theological manual for those seeking to understand the theology of revival. While personal revival is addressed throughout the work, the emphasis of this book is corporate revival. *The Revival Journey* will be a faith builder to all who read it with an open heart.

To order visit www.revivalfocus.org.